# Kosher Laughs AND Lessons FOR Life

**VOLUME III**

MOSAICA PRESS

# Kosher Laughs AND Lessons FOR Life

## 121 AMUSING STORIES AND THOUGHT-PROVOKING LESSONS FOR LIFE

—

### VOLUME III

## YEHOSHUA KURLAND

Published by Mosaica Press, Inc.
www.mosaicapress.com
info@mosaicapress.com

In loving memory of my beloved sister

## Rochel bas Harav Chizkiyahu Yaakov, z"l

# Shelley Kurland, a"h

**1948–2020**

My beloved sister, Shelley Kurland, of blessed memory, was a "special child." In those days (1948), they referred to her as "slow" or "mentally retarded." Anyone who had the merit to know Shelley knew that she was indeed "special." She was a pure spirit who infused hundreds of people with strength and encouragement. She complimented everyone she met with, "you look so beautiful/handsome," a vibrant smile, and obvious love for all others.

Shelley was special because during a time when parents often opted not to raise "special children" at home, my parents, Rabbi Yaakov and Miriam Kurland, never considered that option, and Shelley was raised like every other member of our family. In a home that exuded Torah values and hospitality, Shelley absorbed the sweetness of the Torah and a love for people of all stripes. To my parents' credit, they were always b'simchah about their situation. With tremendous bitachon, they went on to have three other children (Shelley was the oldest), and gave longevity to what was expected in those times to be a shortened existence (Shelley lived seventy-two years).

But more than that, they encouraged her personality to develop. So with great charm and an unusual memory, Shelley delighted and raised the spirits of the hundreds with whom she came into contact in Baltimore, Maryland, where we grew up; in Hicksville, Long Island, where my father served as a rav; in Far Rockaway, New York, in particular the Sh'or Yoshuv community, where I have been blessed to teach for the past forty-five years; and in the Beis Ezra Women's Home on East 18th Street in Brooklyn, which took such good care of her for the past twenty-four years.

She was "the address" for the many Shabbos visits and ensuing games and fun that would follow for countless Bais Yaakov girls in Baltimore, and the T.A.G. and B'nos Bais Yaakov girls in Far Rockaway. Then there were the many gracious people whose homes she would visit on a regular basis. Songs were sung, including the famous "Shelley Is a Friend of Mine" and hundreds of other Jewish songs that she perfected in her hours and hours of listening to records and tapes (she knew every note of Carlebach's "Mimkomcha").

She was the first to stand up and speak at every Shabbos seudah and simchah, always encouraging the yeshiva bochurim at our table to "learn more Torah," and always instructing them, "don't play so much checkers." I imagine this was her way of discouraging the sichas yeladim (playfulness of youth) that is so consuming. She said it all with great exuberance and excitement, as it came from a pure neshamah and a ruach tehorah (pure spirit).

A close friend once told me that it took nine tries before she successfully passed her driving test and got her driver's license; she wanted to give up many times along the way. But it was Shelley who gave her the encouragement not to give up, telling her that she could do it, that ultimately helped her to persevere.

Shelley loved to go to shul and sing along with the chazan (cantor) without reservation. She was one of the first to dance with the kallah (bride) at a wedding—sometimes before the immediate family, sharing in everyone's simchah even if it would never be her own. It didn't matter to someone so purely selfless. In her inimitable style, she addressed everyone by their first name, which rang out with her absolute love and devotion. Her simchas hachayim was contagious and her constant outpouring of berachos to others was rebbe-ish, as if she were responding to the requests in a kvittel. She somehow knew what people needed and never disappointed them.

Our love for Shelley knew no bounds. She told me so often that I was her favorite brother (of course, I'm her only brother). Shelley, I hope you knew that you were everyone's favorite sister and friend, without exception. No words can ever express who you were and what you represented to so many. This is a meager attempt. You will always be my special sister, Shelley, special to me and exceptional to the world you created. I love you eternally.

It is with all of this in mind, and so much more, that I dedicate this book, Kosher Laughs and Lessons for Life, Volume 3, to your memory. You made hundreds smile with your great sense of humor, and at the same time, you taught them invaluable lessons for life that they will never forget. We will never forget you.

ת.נ.צ.ב.ה.

*Your brother who loves you dearly,*
*Yehoshua Kurland*

In tribute
to the memory of

*R' Dovid ben R' Yosef, z"l*

## Mr. David Weinberg

of blessed memory

and

*R' Pinchus ben R' Nosson Chanoch Hakohein, z"l*

## Mr. Fred Gross

of blessed memory

(father and father-in-law of my dear friends
Jeff and Sharona Weinberg)

Two refined and aristocratic gentlemen
who appreciated a good laugh.
But more importantly, they served as eternal role models
for many valuable lessons in life to all who knew them.

May their merit accompany their children
in all of their endeavors.

.ת.נ.צ.ב.ה

# Table of Contents

## Legacy
65 Dogmatism. . . . . . . . . . . . . . . . . . . . . . . . . . . . . . . . . . . . . .73
66 "Hairloom". . . . . . . . . . . . . . . . . . . . . . . . . . . . . . . . . . . . .74

## Manipulation
67 The Numbers Game. . . . . . . . . . . . . . . . . . . . . . . . . . . . . .75

## Marriage
68 Behind Every Boss Is the Boss. . . . . . . . . . . . . . . . . . . .77
69 Never Wrong . . . . . . . . . . . . . . . . . . . . . . . . . . . . . . . . . . .78
70 Incarceration . . . . . . . . . . . . . . . . . . . . . . . . . . . . . . . . . .78
71 The Ham Sandwich. . . . . . . . . . . . . . . . . . . . . . . . . . . . .79
72 Enduring Adulation. . . . . . . . . . . . . . . . . . . . . . . . . . . . .80

## Maturity
73 The Magic Penny . . . . . . . . . . . . . . . . . . . . . . . . . . . . . . .81

## Messages
74 Next Text . . . . . . . . . . . . . . . . . . . . . . . . . . . . . . . . . . . . .82

## Mistakes
75 Superfluous Redundancy . . . . . . . . . . . . . . . . . . . . . . . .83

## Modesty
76 Extra! Extra! Read All About It!. . . . . . . . . . . . . . . . . . .84

## Money
77 The Divine Dollar. . . . . . . . . . . . . . . . . . . . . . . . . . . . . . .85

## Old Age
78 Doctor's Orders . . . . . . . . . . . . . . . . . . . . . . . . . . . . . . . .86

## Old Fashion
79 Discarded . . . . . . . . . . . . . . . . . . . . . . . . . . . . . . . . . . . . .87

## Parents
80 Gotta Love Mom . . . . . . . . . . . . . . . . . . . . . . . . . . . . . . .88

## Perfection
81 Just Getting By. . . . . . . . . . . . . . . . . . . . . . . . . . . . . . . . .90

# Preface

With much thanks to G-d in heaven and recognition of His constant flow of kindness, I have been privileged to publish an eleventh book that utilizes humor as a tool to inspire the assimilation of important life-impacting messages, *Kosher Laughs and Lessons for Life, Volume 3*.

As a teacher of Talmudic law and Jewish ethics for the past forty-five years at the Sh'or Yoshuv Rabbinical College in Far Rockaway, New York, and as an educator and public speaker and lecturer, I have seen the value of utilizing the universal language of humor to help establish a rapport with my audience, and hopefully, open up their hearts and minds to the lesson being taught. My goal has been to inspire others to contemplate their course in life in a way that will maximize their productivity and actualize the vast potential within them. Given the protective walls that surround most people's hearts, it is difficult to penetrate and reach their souls. But with the help of a humorous story that serves as a bit of an allegory and has a soothing, heart-opening effect, their barriers are pierced and people become more open to the important lessons that follow.

As in the first two volumes of *Kosher Laughs and Lessons for Life*, in an attempt to capitalize on the advantages of a "quick fix," I have abandoned extensive serious essays in favor of a joke followed by a few simple lines conveying its lesson. I pray that this collection of humorous stories, along with these contemplative thoughts, will inspire a response of introspection and reflection concerning the topic at hand or prompt the reader to compose his own additional lesson.

My heartfelt thanks go to my wonderful friends Seth and Zahava Farbman of Woodmere, New York, for their unwavering support and generosity in helping to make this book a reality. I thank them both for partnering with me in this and other endeavors, and for providing the impetus to actualize my literary aspirations. They are people blessed with a wonderful sense of humor, but more importantly, they are growth enthusiasts who are constantly looking to stretch and improve themselves. Seth and Zahava, you never cease to amaze me with your myriad good deeds, and I have gained immeasurably from our friendship. Thank you for always being there for me. May you and your family be blessed with all of G-d's blessings.

My heartfelt thanks as well go to my dear friends, Jeff and Sharona Weinberg, who are always willing and ready to help sustain my projects. Thank you for your encouragement and friendship. You are very dear to my heart and I wish you great joy from all of your lovely children. It is a personal honor for me that this new volume is in tribute to your beloved fathers, of blessed memory, Mr. David Weinberg and Mr. Fred Gross. May they be *meilitzei yosher* (advocates in the Heavenly court) on your behalf and on behalf of your extended family.

My appreciation is also boundless to Rabbi Yaacov Haber and Rabbi Doron Kornbluth of Mosaica Press; Mrs. Sherie Gross, managing editor; and their extremely efficient staff, for once again understanding my intent, encouraging this project, and for producing a high-quality work.

As always, there are no words to express my heartfelt love and appreciation for my wife, Leah, and all of my wonderful children. They have brought me endless joy in life and much reason to reflect on all of G-d's blessings through their magnificent example.

Last, but certainly not least, I dedicate this book to my beloved sister, Shelley, *a"h*, who was taken from us along with so many others during this devastating pandemic. She was a pure soul who felt only love for people and love for Hashem, and she infused her world with joy.

There are never enough words to properly express all my appreciation. It is my hope that my words here conveyed my intentions.

With my unceasing thankfulness to Hashem for all of His goodness, and with a prayer that my "light" approach to the topics in this volume will produce much light in turn and help illuminate Your world, I am sincerely yours,

Yehoshua Kurland
18th of Cheshvan 5781

# Anguish

# 1 DISAPPOINTMENT

A man sitting in a bar saw a friend at a table, drinking alone. Approaching the friend, he commented, "You look terrible. What's the matter?"

"My mother died in August," his friend answered, "and left me $25,000."

"Gee, that's tough," the man commiserated.

"Then in September," his friend continued, "my father died, leaving me $90,000."

"Wow! Two parents gone in two months. No wonder you're depressed."

"Then last month, my aunt died," continued his friend, "and left me $15,000."

"Three close family members lost in three months? How sad that is!" said the man.

*"Then this month," his friend dejectedly continued, "so far there's been absolutely nothing!"*

**When one's heart is in anguish, he needs to talk it over with a friend who is a good listener. Half the battle is to share the worry and thereby reduce its intensity. The other half of the battle might very well be a resolution suggested. Whatever you do, don't hold it inside.**

# *Appreciation*

## 2 AND KEEP THE CHANGE

A Chinese doctor moved to the United States and couldn't find a job in a hospital, so he opened his own clinic and put up a sign outside. It read: "GET TREATMENT FOR $20—IF NOT CURED, GET $100 BACK."

A lawyer passed by and saw the sign. He thought this was a great opportunity to make a nice profit so he went inside.

> LAWYER: "I've lost my sense of taste."
>
> DOCTOR: "Nurse, bring the bottle of medicine from box no. 22 and put three drops in this patient's mouth."
>
> LAWYER: "Ugh, this tastes like kerosene!"
>
> DOCTOR: "Congratulations! You're right and I see your sense of taste is restored. Pay me $20."

*A few days later, the angry lawyer returned to recover his money.*

LAWYER: *"I've lost my memory. I can't remember a thing."*

DOCTOR: *"Nurse, bring the bottle of medicine from box no. 22 and put three drops in this patient's mouth."*

LAWYER (ANNOYED): *"But it isn't medicine. It's kerosene. You gave it to me the last time I was here to restore my taste."*

DOCTOR: *"Congratulations! You got your memory back. Pay me $20."*

*The fuming lawyer paid him and then came back a week later, determined to get $100 this time.*

LAWYER: *"My eyesight has become very weak. I can't see at all.*

DOCTOR: *"Well, I don't have any medicine for that, so take this $100."*

LAWYER (STARING AT THE NOTE): *"But this is $20, not $100!"*

DOCTOR: *"Congratulations! Your eyesight is restored. Give me back the $20."*

**If we would have to pay for the gift of our senses, the bill would be exorbitant. Truth be told, we may not owe money, but we certainly owe gratitude. We must never take our senses for granted; we should continuously express our heartfelt appreciation to the Source of these precious life-sustaining gifts.**

# *Between Man and G-d*

## 3 CREATION

*An atheistic scientist came to G-d and said, "We've figured out how to make a man without you."*

*G-d replied, "Okay, let me see you do it."*

*So the atheist bent down to the ground and scooped up a handful of dirt. But G-d stopped him and said, "Oh, no you don't. Get your own dirt!"*

And what exactly did you come from, sir? And what will you return to after you are no longer alive? All of it belongs to your Creator. You can't possibly accomplish anything without Him, because you are using the very things He created.

# 4 INJUSTICE

*Immediately upon the passing of US Supreme Court Justice Ruth Bader Ginsburg, Hillary Clinton called President Donald Trump and offered to replace her.*

*The President responded, "That would be fine with me, but I think you'll have to call the funeral parlor and ask them!"*

**As much as we are aware of our mortality, we, nonetheless, live in denial about the reality that it isn't always someone else—and we therefore better shape up without delay.**

# 5 HEAVENLY SURPRISES

*On their way to get married, a young Catholic couple was involved in a fatal car accident. The couple then found themselves sitting outside the Pearly Gates, waiting for the angel to come and process them into heaven. While sitting there, they began to wonder: could they possibly get married in heaven? When the angel showed up, clipboard in hand, they asked him.*

*The angel responded, "I don't know. This is the first time anyone has asked that. Let me go and find out."*

*The couple sat and waited and waited. Two months passed and the couple was still waiting. With so much time to think, they began to wonder what would happen if it didn't work out. Could one get a divorce in heaven?*

*After yet another month, the angel finally returned, looking somewhat bedraggled. "Yes," he informed the couple, "you can get married in heaven."*

*"Great!" enthused the couple. "But we were just wondering, what if things don't work out? Can we also get a divorce in heaven?"*

*The angel, red-faced with anger, slammed his clipboard onto the ground.*

*"What's wrong?" asked the frightened couple.*

*"OH, COME ON!" the angel shouted. "It took me three months to find a priest up here to marry you! Do you have any idea how long it'll take me to find a lawyer?"*

**Heaven will be filled with simple people who did the bidding of their Creator just because it was His will—no questions asked, no lengthy deliberations. This is called faith—unadulterated belief in the One Above.**

# 6 INSCRIBED

*In a Catholic school's cafeteria, a nun put a note in front of a pile of apples. It read, "Take one only. G-d is watching."*

*Farther down the line was a pile of cookies. A little boy wrote his own note and put it there. It read, "Take all the cookies you want. G-d is watching the apples."*

**There is nothing He doesn't see or know. You aren't fooling anyone! If you like cookies, enjoy them; but remember to bless G-d. He is definitely listening.**

# 7 MIDLIFE CRISIS

*One day, a fifty-four-year-old woman had a heart attack and was taken to the hospital. It was determined that she needed immediate open-heart surgery. While on the operating table, she had a near-death experience. Seeing G-d, she asked, "Is this the end for me?"*

*G-d replied, "No, you have another thirty-four years to live."*

*Upon her recovery, the woman decided to stay in the hospital and undergo a face-lift, liposuction, and a tummy tuck. She even changed her hair color and style as well. The woman released from the hospital looked much younger than the one who entered.*

*Soon after, while crossing the street on her way home, she was run over by a truck. In heaven, she stood in front of G-d and complained, "You said I had another thirty-four years to live. Why didn't you save me from the truck?"*

*G-d replied, "You've got to be kidding! That was you? I didn't recognize you!*

**More importantly, in what shape is the soul that we return to Him after 120 years? Will G-d even recognize it? Did we allow our physical being to control its spiritual counterpart? Or did our soul soar to new horizons after we overcame temptation and were guided by the will of our Creator?**

# Between Man and His Fellow Man

## 8 APPROBATION

Upon his return home from college for Thanksgiving, Jeremy was about to ring the bell when he remembered the two sweaters—the gray one and the red one—that his mother had sent him for his birthday. With a mad dash to his car, he found the gray one in his suitcase and promptly put it on. Proud of his sensitivity, he rang the bell and his mother opened the door.

"Jeremy," she exclaimed, "so nice to see you! What's the matter? You don't like the red one?"

A wise man once said, "I can't tell you the key to success, but the key to failure is trying to please everyone." Without a doubt, it is hard to please everyone, and sometimes outright impossible. Nonetheless, we aim to please and help out others the best we can, for we live by the rule that by doing so, we lose nothing and have everything to gain.

# 9  INGENIOUS

*A proud and confident genius made a bet with a simple-minded fellow. The genius said, "Hey, every question I ask you that you don't know the answer to, you have to give me $5. And if you ask me a question and I don't know the answer, I'll give you $5,000."*

*The simple-minded fellow nodded and said, "Okay."*

*The genius then asked, "How many continents are there in the world?" The simple-minded fellow didn't know and handed over $5.*

*Next it was the simple-minded fellow's turn. "Now let me ask: what animal stands with two legs but sleeps with three?"*

*The genius wracked his brain for the answer but eventually gave up and handed over $5,000. Shaking his head, he said, "I can't believe I lost. By the way, what was the answer to your question?"*

*The simple-minded fellow handed over $5.*

Never underestimate anyone. Everyone has his moment of glory. Once we arrive at the world of souls, we will likely be shocked to see how far back our seats are, while that "simple-minded fellow" sits in the first row.

# 10 WISHFUL THINKING

*Three friends stranded on a desert island found a magic lamp.
Inside it was a genie who agreed to grant each friend one wish.*

*"I want to go home," said the first friend. The genie granted her wish.*

*"I want to go home too," said the second friend. So the genie also
sent her back home.*

*"I'm lonely," said the third friend. "I sure wish my friends were
back here."*

**When one loves his friend as he loves himself and wishes
him well, it must be with selflessness, objectivity, and
certainly not to benefit himself.**

# Between Man and Himself

# 11 YOU WON'T BELIEVE THIS

The presidential election was too close to call. Neither the Republican candidate nor the Democratic candidate had enough votes to win. There was much talk about ballot recounting, court challenges, etc., but a week-long ice fishing competition seemed the most sportsmanlike way to settle things. The candidate who caught the most fish by the end of the week would win the election.

After much back and forth discussion, it was decided that the contest would take place on a remote frozen lake in northern Minnesota. There were to be no observers present, and both men were to paddle to separate parts of this isolated lake and return at 5 p.m. with their catch for counting and verification by a team of neutral individuals.

*At the end of the first day, Donald Trump returned with ten fish. Soon thereafter, Joe Biden returned with no fish. Everyone just assumed he was having a bad day or something, and that he would catch up the next day.*

*At the end of the second day, Donald Trump came in with twenty fish and Joe Biden again came in with none.*

*That night, Nancy Pelosi met secretly with Joe Biden and said, "Joe, I think Trump is a low-life cheat. I want you to go out tomorrow and don't even bother with fishing. Just spy on him and see how he's doing it."*

*The next night (after Donald Trump returned with fifty fish), Nancy asked Biden, "Tell me, Joe, how is Trump cheating?"*

*Biden replied, "Nancy, you're not going to believe this, but he's cutting holes in the ice!"*

**Just like we can't gain access to our computers without a password, so too we will never understand our inner powers without gaining access. As a result, we will remain untapped and sadly unused. Access comes from serious introspection and contemplation of life. There are a lot of fish in the lake for the one who breaks through the ice.**

# 12 INDIVIDUALITY

*A woman gave birth to twins and gave them up for adoption. One of them went to a family in Egypt and was named Ahmal. The other went to a family in Spain and they named him Juan.*

*Years later, Juan sent a picture of himself to his birth mother. Upon receiving the picture, she told her husband that she wished she also had a picture of Ahmal.*

*Her husband responded, "But they're twins! If you've seen Juan, you've seen Ahmal."*

**No two people are the same: not in appearance, not mentally, and not spiritually. As a matter of fact, this also holds true for the entirety of creation. Given man's uniqueness, his task in life can be fulfilled by none other than he, and his contribution to the world is thereby invaluable and irreplaceable.**

# 13 LIVING LIFE TO ITS FULLEST

*On the first day, G-d made the dog and said, "Sit all day by the door of your house and bark at anyone who comes in or walks past. For this, I will give you a life span of twenty years."*

*The dog said, "That's a long time to be barking. How about only ten years and I'll give you back the other ten?" So G-d agreed.*

*On the second day, G-d created the monkey and said, "Entertain people, do tricks, and make them laugh. For this, I'll give you a twenty-year life span."*

*The monkey said, "Monkey tricks for twenty years? That's a pretty long time to perform. How about I give you back ten years like the dog did?" And G-d agreed.*

*On the third day, G-d created the cow and said, "You must go into the field with the farmer all day long and suffer under the sun, have calves, and give milk to support the farmer's family. For this, I will give you a life span of sixty years."*

*The cow said, "That's kind of a tough life you want me to live for sixty years. How about giving me twenty and I'll give back the other forty?" And G-d agreed once again.*

*On the fourth day, G-d created man and said, "Eat, sleep, play, and enjoy your life. For this, I'll give you twenty years."*

But man said, "Only twenty years? Could you possibly give me my twenty, the forty the cow gave back, the ten the monkey gave back, and the ten the dog gave back? That makes eighty, okay?"

"Okay," said G-d, "you asked for it."

So that is why for our first twenty years we eat, sleep, play, and enjoy ourselves. For the next forty years, we slave in the sun to support our family. For the next ten years, we do monkey tricks to entertain the grandchildren. And for the last ten years, we sit on the front porch and bark at everyone.

**Until we recognize that we are created in a class that is far superior to the beast, we tend to act like them. We need to tap into our greatness that lies in the fact that we are created in the image of G-d, unlike our animal friends, and emanate from a source close to His holy throne.**

# *Bias*

# 14 SENSELESS AND AGELESS HATRED

After recess, the first grade teacher announced, "I am going to go around the classroom and ask you all what you did during recess. If you can write what you did on the board, you'll get a lollipop."

The first girl asked was Jessica. "Jessica, what did you do during recess?"

"I played in the sand box."

"Okay," said the teacher, "let me see you write the word box on the board." Jessica did and got a lollipop.

Next was Tom. "I played with Jessica in the sand box."

"Okay, let me see you write the word sand on the board," said the teacher. He did and got a lollipop.

The next one was David Goldberg. "Well," David said, "I tried to play in the sand box, but Jessica and Tom threw rocks at me."

*"What?" the teacher exclaimed. "They threw rocks at you? That sounds like outright, unequivocal anti-Semitism to me. Let me see you write outright, unequivocal anti-Semitism on the board and you'll get a lollipop."*

**It is terribly sad when people are judged by their race, color, or creed. We need to champion good over evil—admire the former and detest the latter. Without this, any other kind of judgment is likely to reek of bias, subjectivity, and stereotypical thinking.**

# *Change*

## 15 BONUS POINTS

*"I'm not interested in any diet plan unless it lets me use rollover calories."*

Diets are just one example of how old habits are hard to break. Everyone is looking for a bonus and a head start. But the truth is that for a diet to work successfully, eating behavior must be changed. Otherwise, the calories and pounds will indeed roll over again and again. This is true for all behavior modification.

# *Character*

## 16 CONFUSED AGAIN

*Right now I'm experiencing amnesia and déjà vu at the same time...I think I've forgotten this before!*

In the ongoing battle for character development, man finds himself trying to juggle many extremes in order to strike the proper balance and ultimately find the happy medium. He who does this joins mankind, the aristocracy of the world, who are a credit to G-d's greatest symphony.

# Charity

# 17 FUNDRAISING?

"Sir, you have got to help!" said the tearful man at the door. "There is a family that I know very well that is in desperate need of money. The father has been out of a job for over a year and they have five kids at home with barely a morsel of food to eat. The worst part is that they are about to be kicked out of their house, and they will be left on the streets without a roof over their heads," the man concluded with one last heart-wrenching sob.

"Well," said the man who had opened the door, "that really is a sad story. Why don't you come inside and we'll talk about it a little more."

"So how much money is needed exactly?" the man continued once they were both seated.

"Oh, it's really terrible," the soliciting man started up again. "Why just for the rent, $3000 is needed by tomorrow. Otherwise they'll be kicked out onto the streets."

*"How do you know so much about this situation?" the other man
asked as he reached for his checkbook.*

*"Well," said the man, breaking down once more, "they're my tenants."*

King Solomon wrote, "Charity saves one from death."
The generous donor looks at himself and his wealth and
considers himself merely to be an emissary of the One
above, Who entrusted him with financial abundance.

# *Children*

# 18 BOXED IN

*Driving with my two young boys to a funeral, I tried to prepare them by talking about burial and what we believe happens after death. The boys behaved well during the service. But at the gravesite, I discovered my explanations weren't as thorough as I'd thought.*

*In a loud voice, my four-year-old asked, "Mom, what's in the box?"*

**Our children deserve the clearest and most articulate explanations of life's many vicissitudes in a thought-out and age-sensitive fashion. They look to us for guidance and they are more resilient than we think. We should never disappoint them.**

# 19  CONGRATULATIONS

*Four men were in a hospital waiting room while their wives were having babies. A nurse went up to the first guy and said, "Congratulations! You're the father of twins."*

*"That's odd," answered the man. "I work for the Minnesota Twins!"*

*Another nurse came and said to the second guy, "Congratulations! You're the father of triplets!"*

*"That's weird," answered the second man. "I work for the 3M company!"*

*The third man was told by a nurse, "Congratulations! You're the father of quadruplets!"*

*"That's strange," he answered. "I work for the Four Seasons hotel!"*

*The last man began groaning and banging his head against the wall. "What's wrong?" the others asked him.*

*"I work for 7 Up!"*

**With all due respect for the dedication and toil necessary in child rearing, especially in large families, let us never forget that children are the greatest gift we could ever imagine. In a generation that has become so insensitive to the value of human life, we need to appreciate it even more so.**

# 20  SURPRISE VISIT

*Don't ever pay a surprise visit to a child in college. You might be the one getting the surprise. I learned this the hard way when I swung by my son's campus during a business trip. Locating what I thought was his fraternity house, I rang the doorbell.*

*"Yeah?" a voice called from inside.*

*"Does Dylan Houseman live here?"*

*"Yup," the voice answered. "Leave him on the front porch like always. We'll drag him in later."*

**Although we cannot police our children and we must allow them their time and space to develop on their own, nonetheless, a parent is always a parent and must make the effort to be aware of what goes on in their children's lives at any age.**

# 21 YOU BETTER EAT YOUR VEGETABLES

*A bit flustered, I asked my wife, "Honey, the kids don't want to eat their vegetables. What do you want me to do?"*

*She shouted back from the other room, "That's fine, dear. Just throw them out."*

*A little later, I told the children, "Look, I'm just as surprised as you are!" and helped them pack their suitcases...*

**We may be a throw-away society, but we can't throw out our kids and we certainly don't want them to feel that we'd like to. It is unfortunate that some view their children as an imposition when they are truly life's greatest gift, to be cherished forever.**

# 22 WANTED

*A well-known comedian once said, "When I was a kid, I got no respect. I told my mother, 'I'm gonna run away from home.'"*
*She answered, "On your mark..."*

**We are making a big mistake if we think that children don't need to be respected. Every person, according to his age and stature, needs to feel that he is esteemed and valued. More than that, there is much to be learned from children, and when we take the time to do so, they become our teachers.**

# *Concern*

# 23 PSYCHOSIS

*When I was young, I was so self-conscious. Every time football players went into a huddle, I thought they were talking about me.*

On the one hand, thinking that everyone is talking about you can be indicative of a grave psychological illness. On the other hand, thinking that no one cares enough to talk about you can be very depressing. Care for others and they will care for you.

# *Contentment*

## 24 INFERIORITY COMPLEXION

*I had plenty of pimples as a kid. One day I fell asleep in the library. When I woke up, a blind man was reading my face.*

The insecurities felt by a teenager because of pimples can carry on into adult life if they don't come to terms with the well-known dictum of the Sages, "Who is wealthy? The one who is content with his portion."

# *Decadence*

## 25 CLIMBING THE WALLS

*Two factory workers were talking. One man said, "I'm going to make the boss give me the day off."*

*The other man replied, "And how are you going to do that?"*

*"Just wait and see," the first man said. Then he climbed up the wall and hanged himself upside down from the light fixture on the ceiling.*

*The boss came in and exclaimed, "What are you doing?!"*

*The first man replied, "I'm a light bulb."*

*The boss then said, "You've been working so hard that you've gone crazy. I think you need to take the day off." And so, the first man left for the day.*

*The second man started to follow the first, which led the boss to exclaim, "Hey, where do you think you're going?"*

*The second man answered, "I'm going home too. I can't work in the dark."*

One person's imagination can become another person's reality. Darkness spreads that way. Before you know it, it has spiraled out of control. We need to keep the lights on.

# Denial

## 26 INSANITIES

*Two cows were standing in a field. One cow said, "Hey, did you hear about that outbreak of mad cow disease? It makes cows go completely insane!"*

*The other cow replied, "Good thing I'm a helicopter."*

**Recognition and awareness of the problem is half the battle. The other half is the willingness to fix it. Denial is the enemy.**

# Education

## 27 CARD SHARK

*The teacher asked little Johnny if he knows his numbers.*
*"Yes," he replied. "My father taught me."*
*"Good. What comes after three?"*
*"Four," answered the boy.*
*"What comes after six?*
*"Seven," was his quick response.*
*"Very good," said the teacher. "Your dad did a good job. And what comes after ten?"*
*"Jack."*

Kids are exposed to so much so soon; with or without our knowledge, incidentally or deliberately, environmentally and straightforwardly. The purity and innocence of youth has been lost to a licentious world so unabashed that

children are unsheltered and inundated. This is most
unfortunate.

# 28  AS EASY AS APPLE PIE

*A hillbilly family's only son saved up money to go to college. After
about three years, he came back home.*

*They all were sitting around the dinner table, when the dad said,
"Well son, you done gone to college, so you must be perty smart. Why
don't you speak some math fer' us?"*

*"Okay, Pa." The son then said, "Pi R squared."*

*After a moment, the dad said, "Why son, they ain't teached ya
nothin'! Pie are round, cornbread are square."*

**We send our kids to university without really knowing what
they will learn and who they might learn it from. We have
to hope that we have given them the moral fiber to provide
the backbone they will need to weather the storm.**

# 29  STUDENT TEACHING

TEACHER: *Jill, give me a sentence beginning with I.*

JILL: *I is…*

TEACHER: *No, Jill. It's always "I am…"*

JILL: *Okay. I am the ninth letter of the alphabet.*

**In the vernacular of the Sages of the Talmud, "I've learned
much from my teachers and from my colleagues, but more**

than I've learned from them, I have learned from my students."

# 30 THE FUTURE SELF

*When I was a kid, my teacher told me I could be anyone I wanted to be. Turns out identity theft is a crime.*

Predicting the future is not in our power, as we are not prophets. But one thing is for sure: every child has enormous potential within and needs to be encouraged to strive for his unique greatness. That is our task as teachers. The most extreme violation of identity theft is neglecting to tap into that which is within us and trying to be someone else.

# 31 TRASHED

*One day, Jimmy came home early from school and his mom asked, "Why are you home so early?"*

*He answered, "Because I was the only one in the class who answered a question."*

*She said, "Wow! I'm so proud! My son is a genius. What was the question?"*

*"The question was: who threw the trash can at the principal's head?" Jimmy replied.*

With some questions there are no answers, and with others, it might be better not to know the answer.

Regardless, there is much to be gained in asking questions because they expand horizons and inspire contemplation. A good question is invaluable in the learning process.

# *Energy*

# 32 THE YOUNG COUPLE

*Two oldies got engaged, and as they were strolling down the street, excitedly planning their wedding, they passed a drugstore.*

*"Excuse me," the man said to the clerk, "do you sell medicine for memory problems?"*

*"Sure," replied the clerk, "all kinds."*

*"Do you sell anti-inflammatory pills for arthritis?"*

*"Yup," replied the clerk.*

*"Wheelchairs, walkers, adult diapers?"*

*"Yeah," replied the clerk, "all kinds."*

*"Okay, excellent," said the man, "because we're getting married next month, and we want to use your store for our wedding registry."*

**The young-at-heart are inspirational, especially in light of the existence of a segment of the younger population who**

act aged beyond their years, without energy and without resolve. May we all be blessed with long years and full days replete with accomplishment.

# *Equality*

## 33 IT'S ALL THE SAME

*Q. What's blue and smells like red paint?*
*A. Blue paint.*

Color is just the exterior. It is the essence that is primary. The world would be a much better place if we learned the lesson of not judging a book by its cover; it's what's on the inside that counts.

# *Eternal Living*

## 34 DOOR-TO-DOOR SERVICE

*A man, obviously stone drunk, walked into a bar and asked for a drink. "Sorry," the bartender answered, "but it looks like you've already had a little too much to drink."*

*Fuming mad, the drunk walked out the front door and back in through the side door. "Can I have a drink please?"*

*"Sorry," the bartender said, "but you can't have a drink here."*

*The drunk walked out the front door and came back in through the back door. "Can I please have a drink?"*

*"Enough!" the bartender screamed. "I told you, NO DRINKS!"*

*The drunk looked closely at the bartender and exclaimed, "Darn! How many bars do you work at?"*

**The alcoholic may not know where he is, but he sure knows what he wants. Many people are non-drinkers and they**

may know where they are, but they have no clue what they want. Those who truly succeed in life are those who know where they are, what they want, where they are headed, and how to get there.

# 35 HARD SHOES TO FILL

*As part of my job as a preschool teacher I have to help the children put on their coats and boots. One day when school was over and the children were getting ready to leave, one child came over to me in tears. "My boots are missing," she wailed.*

*"They're in the corner," I said, pointing to her boots.*

*"Those aren't mine!" she said, stamping her foot. "MINE HAD SNOW ON THEM!"*

Life passes so quickly. Here today, gone tomorrow. And although we cannot hold on to the past and the future is not ours to see, there is one thing we can seize and we dare not let it slip away: the present. Make the most of every precious moment and we can transform our daily routine into eternal benefits.

# 36 KNOCKOUT PUNCH

*Before the surgery, the anesthesiologist offered to knock me out with gas or a boat paddle.*

*It was an ether/oar situation.*

Anesthesiology surely masks the pain in the present but often can cause complications in the aftermath. A difficult choice, but when it comes to physical pain, usually the present wins out. In the realm of the spiritual, as much as we value the present—for every second of life is precious—we need to consider the future as well, for eternal living, not temporal, is the goal.

# 37 LONGEVITY

*You know you're getting old when you get that one candle on your birthday cake. It's like, "See if you can blow this out."*

King David wrote in Psalms, "Don't cast us away nor abandon us to a time of old age when we no longer will have strength." Man's purpose in life is to rise to his challenges and overcome temptation by which he expands and actualizes his true potential. The greater the degree of the challenge, the greater will be the reward in this world and the next.

# 38 MISSING IN ACTION

*My grandmother started walking five miles a day when she was sixty. She's ninety-seven now and we don't know where she is.*

Exercise is a good thing at any age. But when we get caught up in our physical prowess, we can lose sight of the more important religious pursuits, and spiritual atrophy sets in.

Worse than that, we lose our perspective and have no idea where we are and where we are headed.

# 39 SECURITY

*I needed a password eight characters long, so I picked Snow White and the Seven Dwarfs.*

We are in a time of usernames and passwords. Should we ever forget them, we would be locked out of personal information that we have accumulated over a lifetime. To gain entry into the World to Come, we will need a username and a password. The username will be our deeds, and the password, our devotion.

# 40 THE UPS AND DOWNS OF LIFE

*A stingy old lawyer, who had been diagnosed with a terminal illness, was determined to prove wrong the old saying, "You can't take it with you." After much thought and consideration, the old ambulance chaser finally figured out how to take at least some of his money with him when he died.*

*He instructed his wife to go to the bank and withdraw enough money to fill two pillowcases. He then directed her to take the filled pillowcases to the attic and leave them directly above his bed. His plan: When he passed away, he would reach out and grab the pillowcases on his way to heaven.*

*Several weeks after the funeral, the deceased lawyer's wife, up in the attic cleaning, came upon the two forgotten pillowcases stuffed with cash.*

*"Oh, that old fool," she exclaimed. "I knew he should have had me put the money in the basement."*

**It is amazing how intelligent people can live in absolute oblivion about their true state of spiritual affairs, as if they are guaranteed a piece of the afterworld. There is but one guarantee, and that is: one's afterlife is contingent on a life performance that accrues merit in the fleeting and temporary world of our earthly existence. There is much work to do and little time to do it. We dare not delude ourselves.**

# *Family*

## 41 PREPAID

*A man named Marty called his son. "Harry, I have news to tell you. I know it's going to upset you, but I have made up my mind and there is nothing you can do about it. I have decided to divorce your mother."*

*"But Dad, how can that be?" the son asked. "You've been married for forty years, and you always seemed to get along. What happened all of a sudden?"*

*"Son, I have made up my mind and I don't want you to try to convince me otherwise."*

*"Okay," his son responded, "but you must promise me you won't do anything until I come and talk to you in person, and I'm going to ask all of the siblings to fly in as well."*

*"All right, you have my word," said the father, hanging up.*

*"Well," Marty said, turning to his wife, "I got them all to come in for Thanksgiving, and I didn't even have to pay for the tickets."*

When families get together but once a year, it is unlikely that a real closeness exists. Although one does not choose his relatives, the potential closeness of those relationships is priceless. All too often we misconstrue the value of those relationships and allow the "in-law/out-law" cynical view to supersede all else.

# *Fear*

## 42 LOWER MATHEMATICS

*I have a fear of numbers that aren't the ratio of two integers. I know, it's really irrational.*

**Fear is often a result of feeling powerless to control a situation. Truth, faith in G-d, and recognition that nothing is really in our control can help alleviate our apprehension. Let us not forget that when fear takes over, our thinking is anything but rational.**

# *Focus*

## 43 MCSTAKEN

*A man walked into a library and ordered a hamburger and fries. The librarian quietly reprimanded him and said, "Please, sir. This is a library."*

*"I'm so sorry," the man responded in a softer tone. "I'd like a hamburger and fries, please," he whispered.*

You don't get it, do you? The problem is not that one should lower his decibel in a library, but rather that libraries are not fast-food joints. How often do we miss the point, either deliberately or because of lack of focus. The saddest part about it is we lose learning and growth opportunities because we space out when we should "space in."

# *Forces of Evil*

## 44 SURPRISES

*One day Max went to see Carl. Carl had a big swollen nose.*
*"Whoa, what happened, Carl?" Max asked.*
*"I sniffed a brose," Carl replied.*
*"What?" Max said. "There's no B in rose!"*
*"There was in this one!" Carl replied.*

**The most alluring object and fragrant scent could be wrought with danger. Don't be fooled by the glamour. Too often it is evil in disguise.**

# *Forgetfulness*

## 45 PASSED THE BAR

*An elderly looking gentleman (mid-nineties), very well dressed, hair well groomed, great looking suit, flower in his lapel, smelling slightly of a good aftershave, presenting a well-looked-after image, walked into an upscale cocktail lounge.*

*Seated at the bar was an elderly looking lady. The gentleman walked over, sat alongside her, ordered a drink, took a sip, turned to her and said, "So tell me, do I come here often?"*

**Life is filled with experiences that are neither haphazard nor coincidental but come our way to teach invaluable lessons. How sad it is when we allow ourselves to forget or ignore directives that could have saved us from making the same mistake twice.**

# *Freedom*

# 46 AGELESS CELEBRATION

*The 4th of July was coming up, and the nursery-school teacher took the opportunity to tell her class about patriotism.*

*"We live in a great country," she said. "One of the things we should be happy about is that in this country, we are all free."*

*One little boy came walking up to her from the back of the room. He stood with his hands on his hips and said, "I'm not free. I'm four."*

**We are forever grateful that we enjoy the freedom in our democratic society to make our own choices without autocratic interference. Incarceration to the multiplicity of the all-too-available "freedoms" in our "free" society makes that challenge a daunting task.**

# 47 SELF-INCARCERATION

*At the parole hearing, one of the parole board members asked, "Tell me, why should you be released early?"*

INMATE: *It's bec...*

BOARD MEMBER: *Yes?*

INMATE: *I think I have...*

BOARD MEMBER: *Go on.*

INMATE: *May I please finish my sentence?*

BOARD MEMBER: *Sure. Parole denied!*

**As much as man strives for freedom, he often distorts its true meaning and ends up adopting the behavior of the society he finds himself in. In the Western world, freedom often means unrestrained wanton behavior. But true freedom allows man to actualize his lofty potential and to strive for perfection.**

# Free Will

## 48 TESTING

*A man took his sick Chihuahua to the veterinarian and was immediately ushered into an examination room.*

*Soon, a Labrador came in, sniffed the Chihuahua for ten minutes and left. Then a cat came in, stared at the Chihuahua for ten minutes and left. Finally, the doctor came in, prescribed some medicine, and handed the man a bill for $500.*

*"This bill must be a mistake," the man said. "I've only been here for twenty minutes!"*

*"No mistake," the doctor replied. "It's $200 for the lab test, $100 for the medicine, and $200 for the CAT scan."*

**Though we are unaware of it, we are constantly being tested. Will we make the right choices? Will we be discerning? Will we choose right from wrong, good over**

evil, virtue over iniquity? Will we pass the test? Will we win the battle?

# *Generosity*

# 49 CELLMATE

*After a round of golf, several men were in the golf club's locker room, showering and getting changed. Suddenly a mobile phone on one of the benches rang. A man who was nearby picked it up and the following conversation ensued:*

HUSBAND: *Hello?*

WIFE: *Honey, it's me. Are you at the club?*

HUSBAND: *Yes.*

WIFE: *Great! I'm at the mall two blocks from where you are. I just saw a beautiful leather coat. It's absolutely gorgeous! Can I buy it?*

HUSBAND: *What's the price?*

WIFE: *Only $1,000.*

HUSBAND: *Well, okay, go ahead and get it if you like it that much...*

WIFE: *Uh, and I also stopped by the Mercedes dealership and looked at the 2021 models. I saw one I really liked. It's an SLK model. I spoke with the salesman and he gave me a really good price. And since we need to exchange the BMW that we bought last year...*

HUSBAND: *What price did he quote you?*

WIFE: *Only $165,000...*

HUSBAND: *Okay, but for that price I want it with all the options.*

WIFE: *Great! But before we hang up, something else...*

HUSBAND: *What?*

WIFE: *It may sound like a lot, but I decided to drop by the real estate agent this morning. Guess what! I saw that the price on the house we looked at last year went down! Remember? The one with the swimming pool, English garden, acre of park grounds? The beachfront property.*

HUSBAND: *How much are they asking for it now?*

WIFE: *Only $14.5 million—a magnificent price! And I see we have that much in the bank to cover it.*

HUSBAND: *Well then, go ahead and buy it, but just bid up to $14.2 million. Okay?*

WIFE: *Okay, sweetie. Thanks! I'll see you later! You're the best husband in the world!*

HUSBAND: *My pleasure.*

The man hung up and saw the others in the room looking at him with astonishment and derision. Then he raised the hand holding the phone and asked, "Does anyone know who this belongs to?"

As long as it won't cost us a penny, we are the most charitable people in the world. But there really are some unique individuals who graciously share with others that which G-d has given them, at great cost and expense. They are true emissaries of our Father in heaven.

# Greed

## 50  A GRAVE SIN

*The city's miser was on his deathbed. For his last request, he asked to be alone with his lawyer, doctor, and priest.*

*"I know I am going to die soon," he said, "and I would like to take my money with me, so I am going to give each of you $150,000 in cash and I want each of you to make sure the money goes into my coffin."*

*It was a few days after the funeral when, overflowing with guilt, the priest finally confided to the other two that he had put only $100,000 into the coffin.*

*"I'm glad you brought it up," said the doctor, "because I have also been feeling guilty. I only put $80,000 in it."*

*"You people should be ashamed of yourselves," stormed the lawyer, "stealing money like that! Am I the only honest person here? Look at this," he said, pulling out his checkbook and pointing. "I wrote out a check for the full $150,000!"*

Even time-honored last wishes of a dying man can be ignored by the avaricious and the greedy. Unfortunately, where there is self-indulgence, all integrity goes out the window. "What's in it for me" has become the battle cry of all too many.

# *Guilt*

## 51 UNAPOLOGETIC

*My mom could make anybody feel guilty—she used to get letters of apology from people she didn't even know!*

**Excessive guilt can destroy lives, but without shame and accountability, our spirituality is in grave danger. We must strike the balance between destructive guilt and essential culpability.**

# *Hate*

# 52 ANTI-SEMITISM

A Nazi walked into Bern's bar, looked around, and noticed an older Orthodox Jewish man seated at a nearby table.

"Barman," he called out, "a round on me for all your patrons, but not for the old Jewish geezer over there."

While everyone in the bar was receiving their drinks, he looked with a nasty little smile directly at the Jew. Surprisingly, the Jew nodded his head and sent a warm smile back.

The Nazi was somewhat miffed, as this was not the reaction he expected, so he went over to the bar.

"Barman, a second round for everyone but that Jew, and this time take it all from the top shelf," he said, indicating the good stuff.

As the drinks were being distributed, the Nazi looked again at the Jew and saw that he was still smiling back, even more warmly than before.

*"Is that Jew a complete fool or what?" he asked the barman.*

*The bartender responded, "Oh no, my generous friend, that gentleman is my boss, Mr. Bernstein!"*

**We abhor evil and detest evildoers, but never should we hate others simply because they are different from us. Everyone is created in the image of G-d and should be valued accordingly. To hate for no good reason is to disgrace the Master Creator. History has shown time and time again the absolute evil and destructive consequences of baseless hatred, bigotry, and elitism.**

# 53 UNWARRANTED

*A famous comedian of the past once commented, "I told my psychiatrist that everyone hates me.*

*He said I was being ridiculous—everyone hasn't met me yet."*

**Our insecurities are such that we often believe we are disliked and unpopular. Often this is a projection of our own frustrations and disappointments. In other words, we hate ourselves and imagine that others do as well. We are our worst enemies.**

# *Health*

## 54 OVERHEARD AT THE FAIR

LITTLE GIRL: *I want cotton candy!*

MOTHER: *You can have some cotton candy after you eat something healthy.*

LITTLE GIRL: *I want cotton candy now!*

MOTHER: *I said no, you're going to have something healthy first! How about a corn dog and fries?*

**The lesser of two evils is not the conduit to good health in both the physical and spiritual realm alike. A step in the right direction would be a selection free of cholesterol and spiritual plaque.**

# *Heartfelt*

## 55 ABSORBENT

*Q. What do you call someone who goes into the forest and shoots paper towels?*
*A "Bounty" hunter.*

**The true hunter seeks knowledge and allows it to be absorbed into his heart. In turn, his heart will inspire action and deed.**

# *Honesty*

## 56 STIMULUS PACKAGE

*Three contractors bid to fix a broken fence at the White House. One was from New York, another was from Tennessee, and the third was from Minnesota. All three went together with a White House official to examine the fence.*

*The Minnesota contractor took out a tape measure and did some measuring. Then he worked out some figures with a pencil.*

*"Well," he said, "I figure the job will run about $900: $400 for materials, $400 for my crew, and $100 profit for me."*

*The Tennessee contractor also did some measuring and figuring. Then he said, "I can do this job for $700: $300 for materials, $300 for my crew, and $100 profit for me."*

*The New York contractor didn't measure or figure. He just leaned over to the White House official and whispered, "$2,700."*

*The government official, incredulous, whispered back, "You didn't even measure like the other guys! How did you come up with such a high figure?"*

*The New York contractor whispered to him, "$1,000 for me, $1,000 for you, and we hire the guy from Tennessee to fix the fence."*

**The wheeler-dealer may make more money through his manipulative schemes. But in the real world of living, it is the honest broker who comes out on top. Way on top!**

# 57 IT'S POLITICS AS USUAL

*Q. What do you call a lawyer who's gone bad?*
*A. A senator.*

**Politics has always been replete with empty campaign promises and false commitments. In recent years, there's been no sign of shame, guilt, or responsibility for noncompliance. The brazen face of arrogance has replaced the conciliatory face of admission, and the rest is history.**

# *Hospitality*

## 58 EASY ACCESS

*Q. Why do chicken coops have two doors?*
*A. If they had four doors, they'd be chicken sedans!*

The more doors there are, the greater the access. There are people who open all the doors of their home to guests and those in need in the tradition of Abraham. This is becoming a lost art. Let us endeavor to practice "what is mine is yours" instead of "what is yours is mine."

# *Human Nature*

## 59 EVERYONE MAKES MISTAKES

*A clear conscience is usually the sign of a bad memory.*

There isn't a saint in the world who hasn't erred. But the great ones were aware when they did and immediately made amends. To them, life was all about accruing merit and correcting mistakes as they strove for perfection.

# *Human Spirit*

## 60 NO MONKEY BUSINESS

*A child asked his father, "Where did all the people in the world come from?"*

*So his father answered, "Adam and Eve had babies, then their babies became adults and had babies, and so on."*

*The child then went to his mother and asked her the same question.*

*She told him, "We were monkeys; then we evolved to become like we are now."*

*The child ran back to his father and said, "Mom told me the truth! You lied to me!"*

*His father replied, "No, your mom was talking about her side of family."*

**To think that mankind, who is blessed with the ability to intellectualize, verbalize, and articulate—in other**

words, to think and speak—came from monkeys is as preposterous as thinking that cartoons are real life and that Mr. Ed (the horse) could actually talk. The unique abilities that separate man from the animal kingdom are a level beyond and emanate from a very holy place.

# *Influences*

## 61 AMBIANCE

*Q. Did you hear about the new restaurant on Mars?*
*A. The food is great, but there's not much atmosphere.*

It's all about the atmosphere. Good and bad influences stem from the climate in which we allow ourselves. We need to be wise and stay far away from negative influences before they overpower us. If this is true for adults, it is so much more applicable to impressionable youth.

# Internal Struggles

## 62 THE FINAL FIX

*I can't tell the difference between a rose and a dandelion, so when it came time to spruce up my garden, I had no clue which plants to keep and which ones to remove. Until, that is, my mother gave me this handy tip: "Pull them all up. If something comes back, it's a weed."*

Everything in life is a lesson. The weed takeover of many a garden is a metaphor for a human being who allows his evil inclination to flourish. It will be unrelenting and inexorable, and is sure to come back.

# *Joy*

## 63 EQUILIBRIUM

*Doc, I keep having these alternating recurring dreams. First I'm a teepee, then I'm a wigwam, then I'm a teepee, then I'm a wigwam. It's driving me crazy. What's wrong with me?"*

*The doctor replies, "It's very simple. You're two tents."*

There is much reason for one to feel tense, given the pressure cooker, ever-changing world in which we live. Therefore, it is more important than ever to maintain our equilibrium and stay calm in order to weather each storm. The secret formula for this is to count one's blessings and live each day with great joy.

# *Judgmental Thinking*

## 64 BABY POUCHING

"Oh, no!" the kangaroo groaned to her friend, the rabbit. "The forecast calls for rain."

"What's the problem with that?" asked the rabbit. "We could use some rain."

"Sure," the kangaroo said, "but that means my kids will have to play inside all day!"

**Never judge your friend until you've reached his place. Even what seems to be an identical situation can be stressful for one and easy for the other. Judge him accordingly.**

# *Legacy*

## 65 DOGMATISM

A guy sat down in a movie theater and noticed that the man in front of him had brought his dog and it was sitting in the seat next to him. He thought it was unusual, but since he liked dogs, he decided that as long as it was not a distraction, he wouldn't mention it.

The movie started and pretty soon there was a funny part. The dog made some low woofing sounds that sounded like laughter. In a little while, there was a sad part and the dog appeared to be weeping. This continued throughout the film and the man sitting behind the dog was astounded.

When the lights came on, he tapped the dog's owner on the shoulder and told him, "I gotta say, and I know this sounds weird, but it seemed like your dog really enjoyed this movie."

The dog owner looked at the dog and nodded. "I know, it really is weird because he absolutely hated the book."

**The saddest story of all is when our only companions are our dogs, and our aspirations don't focus on the legacy we will leave for our children. This is nothing to bark at!**

# 66 "HAIRLOOM"

*There was a man who lived near a forest. As he grew older and older, he started losing his hair, until one day, on his deathbed, he was completely bald. That day, he called his children to a meeting.*

*He said, "Look at my hair. It used to be so magnificent, but it's completely gone now. My hair can't be saved. But look outside at the forest. It's such a lovely forest with so many trees, but sooner or later they'll all be cut down and this forest will look as bald as my hair."*

*"What I want you to do," the man continued, "is that every time a tree is cut down or dies, plant a new one in my memory. Tell your descendants to do the same. It shall be our family's duty to keep this forest strong."*

*So they did. Each time the forest lost a tree, the children planted a new one, as did their children and their children after them.*

*And for centuries, the forest remained as lush and pretty as it once was, all because of one man and his re-seeding "heir"line.*

**Life is short and there is much to accomplish. As much as we strive to do our best, we cannot finish it all. But we can endeavor to set things in place for the next generation, with a hope and a prayer that they will accomplish even more.**

# *Manipulation*

## 67 THE NUMBERS GAME

*A mathematician, an engineer, and an accountant applied for a job. The interviewer asked all three of them the same questions, but he realized that they all had different answers when presented with an algebraic equation.*

*The mathematician responded by saying, "I can promise you that the answer to this question is 17.3," and he wrote out a lengthy proof.*

*The engineer answered by saying, "It's probably something close to 15, however we can make that 15 plus or minus 3, just to be safe."*

*The last one, the accountant stood up, closed the door, and leaned in close to the interviewer. In a hushed tone, he asked, "How much do you want it to be?"*

Manipulation seems to be the name of the game. Whether in business, politics, law, accounting—and the list goes on—too many have become accustomed to exploitation as a fact of life to the point where they grant it legitimacy. Essentially, it really amounts to abusive behavior, dishonesty, and outright stealing. Otherwise, it's perfectly fine.

# Marriage

## 68 BEHIND EVERY BOSS IS THE BOSS

*The boss of our small company complained during a staff meeting that the workers didn't respect him enough. Trying to change their attitude, he came in the next day with a sign for his door which read, "I am the boss."*

*One of the employees—apparently not appreciating the change—stuck a Post-it Note on the sign. It read, "Your wife wants her sign back."*

The real boss is the one who can communicate, compromise, and commiserate. They are the bosses over their anger and other negative qualities. That's true power!

# 69 NEVER WRONG

*When I married Mr. Right, I didn't know his first name was Always.*

**Good relationships have little to do with being right and much more to do with good listening habits, respect, humility, and compromise—and most importantly—having the courage and character to admit when we are wrong.**

# 70 INCARCERATION

*A woman awoke in the middle of the night to find that her husband wasn't there. She put on her robe and went downstairs to look for him. She found him sitting at the kitchen table with a cup of hot cocoa in front of him. He appeared to be deep in thought, just staring at the wall. She watched as he wiped away a tear from his eye.*

*"What's the matter, dear?" she whispered as she stepped into the room. "Why are you down here at this time of night!?"*

*Her husband looked up from his drink and said, "It's the twentieth anniversary of the day we met." She couldn't believe he remembered, and she too started to tear up.*

*Her husband continued solemnly, "Do you remember twenty years ago when we were introduced to one another? I was twenty and you were only sixteen."*

*Once again, the wife was touched to tears thinking that her husband was so caring and sensitive. "Yes, I do," she replied.*

*Her husband paused. The words were not coming easily. "Do you remember that your father thought you were too young to date a twenty-year-old, and we ignored him, and I even stole his car, and we eloped?"*

*"Yes, I remember," said the wife, lowering herself into a chair beside him.*

*The husband continued, "Do you remember when he caught up with us, he shoved the shotgun in my face and said, 'Either you take good care of my daughter or I'll make sure you spend the next twenty years in prison for kidnapping and theft?'"*

*"I remember that too," she softly replied.*

*He sighed as he wiped another tear away from his cheek and said, "I would have gotten out today."*

**Today, many look at marriage as a loss of their freedom, when in fact it is precisely this complementary relationship of love and mutual respect that allows a person to free himself of the shackles of self-absorption and enter into a merger that allows full expansion and actualization of potential.**

# 71 THE HAM SANDWICH

*A Jewish rabbi and a Catholic priest were good friends. At a picnic one day, the priest was eating a ham sandwich.*

*"You know," he said to his friend, "this ham sandwich is delicious. I know you're not supposed to eat ham, but I don't understand why such a good thing would be forbidden. When will you break down and try it?"*

*To which the rabbi replied, "At your wedding."*

**Marriage is a great institution. The fusion of husband and wife into one unit, committed to sharing their dreams and providing one another with the mutual love and support**

to tackle the vicissitudes of life, is well worth the ongoing effort essential to its success. The slow demise of marriage in our time and the loneliness that people will endure is sad and frightening.

# 72 ENDURING ADULATION

*Thomas was thirty-two years old and he was still single.*

*One day a friend asked him, "Why aren't you married? Can't you find someone who will be a good wife?"*

*Thomas replied, "Actually, I've found many women I wanted to marry, but when I brought them home to meet my parents, my mother didn't like them."*

*His friend thought for a moment and said, "I've got the perfect solution. Find a woman who's just like your mother."*

*A few months later, they met again and his friend asked, "Did you find the perfect woman? Did your mother like her?"*

*With a frown on his face, Thomas answered, "Yes, I found the perfect woman—she was just like my mother. You were right; my mother liked her very much."*

*"Then what's the problem?"*

*"My father didn't like her," Thomas replied.*

Marriages of convenience, not filled with love and admiration, are a sad commentary and diluted version of an institution that once stood for unqualified adulation, giving, and fidelity—an institution that presented mankind with an ideal opportunity in which to fulfill the Golden Rule: "Love your fellow man as you love yourself."

# Maturity

## 73 THE MAGIC PENNY

*We had just finished tucking our five kids into bed when three-year-old Billy began to wail. Turns out, he had accidentally swallowed a penny and was sure he was going to die. Desperate to calm him, my husband palmed a penny that he had in his pocket and pretended to pull it from Billy's ear.*

*Billy was delighted. In a flash, he snatched it from my husband's hand, swallowed it, and demanded, "Do it again!"*

**Do we learn from our mistakes? Unfortunately, we repeat them again and again, foolishly treating behavior that is replete with danger as some childish game that we play well into our adult lives.**

# *Messages*

## 74 NEXT TEXT

*One night, a husband sent a text to his wife. It read, "Hi. I will get home late. Please try and wash all my dirty clothes and make sure you prepare my favorite dish before I return." He did not receive any reply.*

*He sent another text, "And I forgot to tell you that I got a raise. At the end of the month, I'm buying you a new car."*

*This time she texted back, "OMG, really?"*

*Her husband replied, "No, I just wanted to make sure you got the first message."*

G-d sends us numerous messages. Often, we are not listening, nor are we checking for these communications. They are a preemptive attempt to prompt character improvement and spiritual insight. Their purpose is to rehabilitate us. We should always check our messages.

# Mistakes

## 75 SUPERFLUOUS REDUNDANCY

*I bought the world's worst thesaurus yesterday. Not only is it terrible, but it's terrible.*

The repetition of mistakes turns unwitting infringements into purposeful indiscretions. As the behavior repeats itself, it becomes second nature, and no longer is the mistake a simple mistake, but a deliberate violation.

# *Modesty*

## 76 EXTRA! EXTRA! READ ALL ABOUT IT!

*Did you read the news about corduroy pillows?*
*They're making headlines everywhere!*

In the world at large, giant headlines mean great success.
In the world of truth, it is the humble and the modest who
have really made it.

# *Money*

## 77 THE DIVINE DOLLAR

*My wife divorced me for religious reasons. She worshipped money and I didn't have any!*

Worship of the almighty dollar is one of the world's most renowned religions that has perpetuated for centuries and is still going strong. Beware of its grasp! It will control you!

# *Old Age*

## 78 DOCTOR'S ORDERS

*My doctor told me that jogging could add years to my life. I think he was right. I feel ten years older already!*

Many age quickly. The assiduous and devout can't afford to bemoan aging. They are too busy taking advantage of every precious moment in order to actualize their incredible potential and attain their goals in this world and the next.

# Old Fashion

## 79 DISCARDED

*The other day, I got carded at the liquor store. While I was taking out my ID, my old Blockbuster card fell out. The clerk shook his head, said, "Never mind," and rang me up.*

**It may not be cool to be outdated, but it is very cool to hold on to the traditions and customs of one's lineage because they connect him to something real and rich, not superficial and shallow.**

# *Parents*

# 80 GOTTA LOVE MOM

*Three elderly ladies sat around a table, playing bridge and bragging about their sons.*

"My Freddie," said Margaret, "everyone should be so lucky as to have a son like my Freddie. Once a week he brings me a huge bouquet of flowers. And he's constantly taking me out to restaurants to eat. If I so much as hint that I want something, the next morning it's on my doorstep."

"That's very nice about your Freddie," said Gertrude. "But with all due respect, when I think about the way my Sammy takes care of me, it just can't compare. Every morning, as soon as I wake up, he greets me with freshly brewed coffee. Every afternoon, he comes over and cooks me a gourmet lunch, and every evening, he brings me to his house for supper. He truly treats me like a queen."

"Well," said Barbara, "I don't want to make any of you feel bad or anything, but wait till you hear about my Harry. Twice a week he pays someone $200 an hour just so he can lie on their couch and talk to them.

"And who do you think he talks about at those prices?" Barbara asked, with a big, excited smile. "I'll tell you who he talks about! ALL HE TALKS ABOUT IS ME!

**The ideal relationship between children and parents certainly involves the child speaking about his parents. Not on the therapist's couch, but rather in glowing terms from the comfort of his own home, established after having been infused with all their love and confidence.**

# Perfection

## 81 JUST GETTING BY

*What do you call a student who got Cs all the way through medical school?*

*Hopefully, not your doctor!*

**None of us would be satisfied with a medical professional who barely made it through medical school. Not when it comes to our health! We should be even more selective when it comes to our spiritual health and ensure that our environment is conducive to healthy growth and improvement. Our eternity depends on it!**

# Politics

## 82 EXPLOITATIONS

*Q. What is the difference between capitalism and socialism?*

*A. In a capitalist society, man exploits man; in a socialist one, it's the other way around.*

**When the goal is exploitation, even the greatest political doctrine will be perverse. When the goal is sincere benevolence, the simplest doctrine can be redeeming.**

# *Prayer*

## 83 A NAME CHANGER

*A genie asked, "What's your first wish?"*
*Steve answered, "I wish I was rich!"*
*The genie continued, "And what's your second wish, Rich?"*

**Praying is not about getting what you asked for as much as
it is about the creation of a bond between you and G-d.**

## 84 SERVITUDE

*In the foyer of a synagogue, a young boy was looking at a plaque
inscribed with the names of the men and women who had died in
various wars. He asked the rabbi, "Who are these people?"*

*The Rabbi said, "Those are members from our synagogue who died in service."*

*The boy asked, "Which one: the early service or the late service?"*

**To pray simply to fulfill one's obligation does not compare to a prayer said with enthusiasm inspired by the close relationship he is building with his Creator. In the former, one could lose his taste for prayer, undermining this crucial spiritual connection. In the latter, he will look forward to each and every opportunity to converse with G-d.**

# Presumptions

## 85 THAT'S NOT FUNNY!

*My happiness quickly turned to disappointment when I found that*
*all the comic books I ordered were missing the last page.*
*So now I have to draw my own conclusions.*

Although it is generally not a good idea to be presumptuous
and we should judge favorably, sometimes we have no
choice but to be on guard, leery, and defensive. On the one
hand, we try to give the benefit of the doubt; on the other
hand, we must not be naïve and foolhardy. This is just
another of life's many juggling acts.

# *Priorities*

# 86 DEDICATION

Two retired guys were playing golf. One of them was about to swing his golf club when he noticed a funeral procession going by on the street. The man stopped mid-swing, closed his eyes, and said a short prayer.

The other man, who was truly inspired, remarked after clearing his throat, "Wow! That was one of the most beautiful things I've ever seen."

"Well", the other man said, "I was married to her for forty-five years."

**Self-indulgence surely interferes with the rational thinking essential for a person to set a hierarchy of priorities in his life, for then there is but one priority—himself—and all else falls to the wayside.**

# *Procrastination*

## **87** TOPICAL ILLUSION

*A bank robber pulled out a gun, pointed it at the bank teller, and said, "Give me all your money or you're geography!"*

*"The puzzled teller replied, "Didn't you mean to say 'or you're history'?"*

*The robber retorted, "Don't change the subject!"*

**We are great experts in changing the subject. It serves as a tremendous excuse for not dealing with important issues at hand. It can be a prelude to procrastination. It can thwart industriousness and action. It is the lazy man's personal creed.**

# *Purity*

## 88 CRACKED ANIMALS

*A mother and a son came home from the grocery store. The boy immediately emptied out the box of animal crackers onto the kitchen table.*

*His mother asked him, "Why did you do that?!"*

*The boy answered, "My teacher taught us that one should never eat something if the seal is broken, so I'm looking for the seal."*

**Tamper-proof items have long been the norm because there are individuals who would, in fact, tamper and harm. Yet much goes on around us that is morally debilitating without our giving a thought as to its danger to our spiritual health. Isn't that at least of equal concern?**

# 89 SELECTIVE HYGIENE

*A couple walked into a cheap-looking restaurant. As they were about to sit down, they noticed there were crumbs on their seats. After cleaning up the seat and wiping down the table, they sat down. A waitress came over and asked them what they wanted.*

*"I'll just have coffee," said the man.*

*"Me too," said the woman, "and make sure the cup is clean."*

*The waitress returned with their drinks. "Okay," she said, putting down their cups. "Now, which one of you wanted the clean cup?"*

**Who wouldn't prefer a clean cup? People are very particular about their personal hygiene and cleanliness, and yet they subject their souls to every contaminant in the book.**

# *Reality*

## 90 CATFISH

*One day little Johnny dug a hole in his backyard. The next-door neighbor spotted him and decided to investigate.*
*"Hello, Johnny, what are you up to?" he asked.*
*"My goldfish died and I'm gonna bury him," Johnny replied.*
*"That's a really big hole for a goldfish, isn't it?" asked the neighbor.*
*"That's because he's inside your cat!"*

**Reality is not always what the naked eye sees. Sometimes the real picture is buried deep inside and can only be revealed with great contemplation. What we call nature, in reality, is abstract and intangible, for true reality is what lies beneath the surface.**

# *Rebuke*

## 91 NOBODY CORRECTS ME

*I met a guy who was convinced that there were no words in the English language that had more syllables than vowels.*

*I pointed out to him that he was wrong, but he refused to accept criticism.*

**Criticism is never easily accepted. It requires objectivity and a willingness to improve oneself, both of which are lacking in society at large. The wise appreciate any opportunity to improve their character traits. They are eager to expand and stretch themselves, and they welcome all prospects for personal development.**

# 92 THE (YOLK'S) ON YOU

*A wife was making a breakfast of fried eggs for her husband. Suddenly, he burst into the kitchen.*

*"Careful," her husband cried out, "CAREFUL! Put in some more butter! Oh, my gosh! You're cooking too many at once. TOO MANY! Turn them! TURN THEM NOW! You need more butter. Oh, my gosh! WHERE are we going to get MORE BUTTER? They're going to STICK! Careful. CAREFUL! I said be CAREFUL! You NEVER listen to me when you're cooking! Never! Turn them! Hurry up! Are you CRAZY? Have you LOST your mind? Don't forget to salt them. You know you always forget to salt them. Use the salt. USE THE SALT! THE SALT!"*

*His wife stared at him. "What in the world is wrong with you? You think I don't know how to fry a couple of eggs?"*

*The husband then calmly replied, "Of course you do. I just wanted to show you what it feels like when I'm driving."*

**It is very difficult to effectively give rebuke. People are overly sensitive and can't bear to hear criticism. It takes great wisdom to chastise in a way that won't be counterproductive. If somehow the person's misbehavior can be pointed out in an indirect and less threatening manner, then his defenses can be disarmed and he will be more open to what he's hearing.**

# *Repentance*

## 93 IT'S CALLED STEALING

*I'm a kleptomaniac. When it gets really bad, I take something for it.*

**Often we are so caught up in the web of habit that we repeat negative behaviors, unaware that these are the very areas that desperately need correction. The realist recognizes the dilemma and seeks healthy means by which to avoid repeating past mistakes.**

## 94 REPEAT PERFORMANCE

*Two guys were in a bar watching television when the news came on. It showed a guy on a bridge who was about to jump, obviously suicidal.*

*"I bet you $10 he'll jump," said the first guy.*

*"Bet you $10 he won't," said the second guy.*

*Then, the guy on the television closed his eyes and threw himself off the bridge. The second guy handed the first guy the money.*

*"I can't take your money," said the first guy. "I cheated you. The same story was on the five o'clock news."*

*"No, no. Take it," said the second guy. "I saw the five o'clock news too. I just didn't think the guy was dumb enough to jump again!"*

**The suicidal psyche is trapped in a web of depression and hopelessness. Repeated negativity to that degree is very difficult to undo and a reversal of mindset almost impossible. But it can work the other way. If a person decides to do good and repeats that behavior, his streak of consistency will spur him on to do more. Even the sinner can reverse his pattern of behavior by utilizing the very same tool that got him into his mess in the first place.**

# Responsibility

## 95 HE'S GOT THE WHOLE WORLD IN HIS HANDS

*Q. If you have thirteen apples in one hand and ten oranges in the other, what do you have?*
*A. Big hands.*

As the song goes, "He's got the whole world in his hands." That world is the microcosm of the world at large that every person can build or destroy in the course of his achievements in life. The successful man builds a beautiful world with the many gifts G-d has bestowed upon him.

# *Safety*

## 96 CHANCES

*Five out of six people agree that Russian roulette is safe.*

**As much as life is about taking chances, it is more about knowing when not to take a chance. Be careful!**

## 97 TAXI

*Q. What do you call a guy who's had too much to drink?*
*A. A cab.*

**I wouldn't be surprised if denial wasn't one of the leading causes of death. One who values life would never take chances that are risky.**

# *Self-Destruction*

## 98 SELF-AFFLICTION

*I'm allergic to bread, but I eat it anyway. I guess I'm a "gluten" for punishment.*

If man would prioritize properly and really watch both his physical and spiritual health, he would be in a good position in this world and the next. Why would any sane person invite punishment when so clearly it is not worth it?

# Self-Orientation

## 99 POLITICS AS USUAL

*If con is the opposite of pro, is Congress the opposite of progress?*

If progress means thinking of others, then self-serving political gain is indeed a barrier to advancement. Instead, individuals gain, and the populace as a whole loses big time. Contemplate all that could have been achieved for people if politics wasn't so agenda-based.

## 100 PROUD GRANDMOTHER

*"Hi! My name is Gertrude," said the woman to her seatmate on the plane. "It's so nice to meet you! I'm flying to New York for my*

*grandson's third birthday. I'm so excited! I remember when he was just a little baby and now he's already three! It's really hard to believe. He's the most adorable thing you've ever seen!*

*"You know what? Hold on, I think I might have a picture on me. Let me take a look in my purse. Yes, here it is. Just look at him! Isn't he adorable? Do you see his dimple on his left cheek? Simply adorable! I could stare at his picture all day. Oh my, and you should hear him on the phone! He is just the cutest. He says to me in the sweetest voice, "Hi, Grandma!" It just gets me all teary-eyed."*

*After what seemed like two hours for the poor man sitting next to her, Gertrude seemed to realize that perhaps she was talking a bit too much. "You know, I feel terrible! Here I am just talking and talking without letting you get in a word edgewise! Tell me, what do you think about my grandson?"*

**People takes pride in that which is theirs, and rightfully so. But we must not become so wrapped up in ourselves that we forget the other person or simply use him as a means to promote our self-indulgence.**

# 101 THE I'S HAVE IT

*A worldwide survey was conducted by the United Nations. The interviewer would ask but one question: Excuse me, what is your honest opinion about solutions to the food shortage in the rest of the world?*

*The survey was a huge failure.*

*In Africa, they didn't know what food meant.*

*In Eastern Europe, they didn't know what honest meant.*

*In Western Europe, they didn't know what the rest of the world meant.*

*In China, they didn't know what opinion meant.*

*In the Middle East, they didn't know what solution meant.*
*And in Russia, they didn't know what excuse me was.*

**Every place has its own character and attitudes, its own
priorities and agenda, and its own vernacular, but there
is one thing they all share in common: they know what
*yours* means.**

# Sensitivity

## 102 STAR RAGING

*I've been getting into astronomy, so I installed a skylight in my ceiling. The people who live above me are furious.*

People "getting into things" often means they're getting into themselves and being oblivious to their surroundings. And although it is good to feel energized, it should never be at the expense of someone else.

# *Sharing*

## 103 INDIAN GIVER

*In class, Jose was asked to use the word Cherokee in a sentence. He paused and said, "I lost my house key and now I have to Cherokee with my sister."*

There is nothing wrong with sharing. It builds character. It teaches giving and prevents one from becoming a taker. It helps assure that one will be a good husband or wife, a good friend, and a good neighbor.

# Silence

## 104 UNSPEAKABLE

*My wife asked me to pass her lip balm. By mistake, I gave her Krazy Glue instead.*
*She's still not talking to me.*

**We were born with teeth and lips in order to encourage thoughtful and sensitive speech, not garrulous and loquacious rambling. Silence at the right time is a prelude to wisdom.**

# *Society*

## 105 MINDLESS

*If the right side of the brain controls the left side of the body, then lefties are the only ones in their right mind.*

Sometimes you have to wonder if anyone is in their right mind anymore. To suggest that some people are so "open-minded that their brains fall out" is no longer a humorous quip, but a reality. The wise man thinks about the future and sees what might be the consequences of his thoughts and deeds and acts accordingly with vision and perspicacity.

# *Spontaneity*

## 106 IMPROVISATION

*A security guard saw a blind guy walk into a mall with his seeing eye dog. All of the sudden, the guy reached down, grabbed his dog by the tail, and started twirling it around in a circle above his head.*

*The security guard ran over to the guy and screamed, "Put that dog down this instant! That's animal cruelty! What on earth do you think you're doing?"*

*The blind guy replied, "Oh, I'm just looking around."*

So often our expectations are not realistic and we expect state-of-the-art conditions all of the time. It wouldn't even occur to us to improvise. We would do much better and minimize our frustrations if we became more spontaneous and made the best of every situation as it arose.

# *Striving*

## 107 GOING FOR BROKE

*A man walked into a bar and ordered a drink. He noticed that there were pieces of meat nailed to the ceiling of the bar, so he asked the barman what they were for. The barman replied, "If you can jump up and pull one of them down, you'll get free beer all night. If you fail, you have to pay the bar $100. Do you want to have a go?"*

*The man thought about it for a minute before saying, "Nah, the steaks are too high!"*

**When man loses the initiative to strive for greater accomplishments, he wears away G-d's original intentions for humankind and contributes to the legitimization of mediocrity and complacency instead of growth and improvement.**

# *Subjectivity*

## 108 PIPE DOWN

*A Scottish mother visited her son in his New York City apartment and asked, "How do you find the Americans, Donald?"*

*"Mother," said Donald, "they're such noisy people. One neighbor won't stop banging his head against the wall, while the other screams and screams all night long."*

*"Oh Donald, how do you manage to put up with them?"*

*"What can I do? I just lie quietly in my bed, playing my bagpipes."*

**It's easy to blame the next guy! We may be intelligent and astute human beings, but we can be amazingly oblivious and unmindful when we are blinded by our self-preoccupation.**

# *Suspicion*

## 109 I'M BEING FOLLOWED

*A man walked into a library and asked the librarian for books about paranoia.*

*She whispered, "They're right behind you!"*

Believers in a higher authority are well aware of being followed every second of their day by the Eye that sees, the Ear that hears, and the Scribe who records all deeds and misdeeds. Yet this sobering thought is balanced with emotional stability and productivity.

# Sustenance

## 110 'MOO'TUALITY

*Q. What did the mother cow say to the baby cow?*
*A. "It's pasture bedtime."*

**G-d provides for all His creations in the most miraculous way. Pasture to sustain the cow and the like is just one example. Yet for some strange reason, human beings (fools that we are) are convinced that they provide their own sustenance and forget so quickly that "The L-rd is my shepherd..."**

# *Tears*

## 111 FACE THE TRUTH

*My friend thought he was smart. He told me an onion is the only food that makes you cry, so I threw a coconut at his face.*

Tears are a commodity of great value. They break through barriers and make an impression. In prayer, they prove sincerity and authenticity. We pray that our tears will always be joyous; regardless, they can be put to good use.

# *Thankfulness*

## 112 EVERY BREATH COUNTS

*Four elderly men were out golfing.*

*"These hills are getting steeper as the years go by," one complained.*

*"These fairways seem to be getting longer too," said another.*

*"The sand traps seem to be larger than I remember them," said the third.*

*After hearing enough from his senior buddies, the oldest and the wisest of the four of them—at eighty-seven years old—piped up and said, "Just be thankful we're still on the right side of the grass!"*

It is so easy to complain and focus on the negative without a thought about the positive. The truly grateful person doesn't look at life that way. To him, life is always about what he has and never about what he lacks or what his

friend may possess. He is fully cognizant that all he was
blessed with is even more than his portion.

# 113 PHYSICALLY FAT

*A seventy-year-old man talking to his friend on the phone said,
"I feel like my body has gotten totally out of shape, so I got my doctor's
permission to join a fitness club and start exercising. I decided to take
an aerobics class for seniors. I bent, twisted, gyrated, jumped up and
down, and perspired for an hour. But by the time I got my sneakers on,
the class was over.*

We need to be thankful for everything, including the
preliminaries that we always took for granted. Nothing in
life is a given, and we thank G-d for enabling every one of
our limbs and organs to function in the most natural—and
yet miraculous—way.

# *Thievery*

## **114** COLLECTOR'S ITEM

*I was at the art museum recently and asked a worker there if I was allowed to take pictures.*
*He replied, "No, they have to stay on the walls."*

**The greatest work of art ever stolen is the untapped potential in every soul, designed by the Master Artist in His very image—unused and idle, a magnificent gift misappropriated.**

# Togetherness

# 115 SYNTHETIC GATHERINGS

*One evening after dinner, my five-year-old son, Brian, noticed that his mother had gone out. In answer to his questions, I told him, "Mommy went to a Tupperware party."*

*This explanation satisfied him for only a moment. Puzzled, he asked, "What's a Tupperware party, Dad?"*

*I've always given my son honest answers, so I figured a simple explanation would be the best approach. "Well, Brian," I said, "at a Tupperware party, a group of women sit around and sell plastic bowls to each other."*

*Brian nodded, indicating that he understood. Then he burst into laughter. "Come on, Dad," he said. "What is it really?"*

**People gather for all types of occasions: some altruistic, some decadent, and some neutral. Undoubtedly, the most**

meaningful and productive of all assemblages is one that inspires and promotes kindness and compassion, truth, justice, and recognition of the glory of the Source of all we possess.

# Trouble

# 116 LESSONS FOR POSTERITY

One day at the end of class, little Johnny's teacher asked the children to go home and think of a story that teaches a moral. The following day, the teacher asked for volunteers to tell their stories and little Suzy raised her hand and went first.

"My dad owns a farm," she began, "and every Sunday we load the chicken eggs onto the truck and drive into town to sell them at the market. Well, one Sunday we hit a big bump and all the eggs flew out of the basket and onto the road." When the teacher asked for the moral of the story, Suzy replied, "Don't keep all your eggs in one basket."

Little Lucy went next. "My dad owns a farm too. Every weekend we take the chicken eggs and put them in the incubator. Last weekend, only eight of the twelve eggs hatched." Again, the teacher asked for the moral of the story. Lucy replied, "Don't count your chickens before they hatch."

*Next up was little Johnny. "My uncle Ted fought in the Vietnam War, and his plane was shot down over enemy territory. He jumped out before it crashed, but he could only take a case of beer, a machine gun, and a machete with him. On the way down, he drank the case of beer. Then he landed right in the middle of one hundred Vietnamese soldiers. He shot seventy with his machine gun, but then he ran out of bullets! He pulled out his machete and killed twenty more. Then the blade on his machete broke, so he killed the last ten with his bare hands."*

*The teacher looked a little shocked. After clearing her throat, she asked what possible moral there could be to this story.*

*"Well," Johnny replied, "don't mess with Uncle Ted when he's been drinking."*

**With all due respect to Uncle Ted's courage, it's not always wise to attempt to resolve every issue all at once. We view avoiding trouble as a weakness—as an attack on our masculinity—when, in fact, it often it is a sign of great wisdom and strength. Avoidance of certain challenges often is the wisest and safest approach.**

# *Trust*

## 117 LOCK HIM UP

A defense attorney was cross-examining a police officer during a felony trial. "Officer, did you see my client flee the scene?" he asked.

"No, sir," the policeman responded, "but I subsequently observed a person matching the description of the offender running several blocks away."

"Officer, may I ask who provided this description?"

"The officer who responded to the scene," the policeman said.

"A fellow officer provided the description of this so-called offender," the lawyer repeated. "Do you trust your fellow officers?"

"Yes sir, with my life."

"With your life?" the lawyer cynically repeated, trying to undermine the officer's credibility in the eyes of the jury. "Let me ask you this then, Officer. Do you have a locker room in the police station—a room where you change your clothes in preparation for you daily duties?"

*"Yes sir, we do."*

*"And do you have a locker in that room?"*

*"Yes sir, I do," the officer said.*

*"And do you have a lock on your locker?" the lawyer questioned, ready to drive his argument home.*

*"Yes sir."*

*"Now why is it, Officer, if you trust your fellow officers with your life, that you find it necessary to lock your locker in a room you share with those same officers?"*

*Without missing a beat, the policeman responded, "You see, sir, we share the building with a court complex, and sometimes lawyers have been known to walk into that room."*

**Trustworthy people earn our trust, while the unscrupulous get what they deserve. One earns the trust of others with conduct that is clothed in integrity and truth. All else will foster distrust and disdain.**

# *Truth*

## 118 ELECTRIFIED

*I built an electric fence around my property yesterday. My neighbor is dead set against it.*

The greatest shock will come when we will see that the person we deemed a failure and a bore is miles ahead of us in the real world of eternity. There, we will see a topsy-turvy world of truth. Those who we thought were in the lowest echelons will be up front. Others whom we idolized will be in the back.

# 119 PORK PACKAGES

*The head of the vegetarian society just couldn't control himself anymore. He just needed to try some pork to see what it tasted like. So one summer day, he told his members he was going on a vacation.*

*He packed out of town and headed to the nearest restaurant. After sitting down, he ordered a roasted pig and impatiently waited for his delicacy. After just a few minutes, he heard someone call his name, and to his great chagrin, he saw one of his fellow members walking toward him. Just at that same moment, the waiter walked over with a huge platter holding a whole roasted pig with an apple in its mouth.*

*"Isn't that something?" the leader said after only a moment's pause. "All I do is order an apple and look what it comes with!"*

**Many people spend a good part of their lives covering up for their lies and deceit. It can come to a point where the truth can no longer be recognized because it has been so well camouflaged and denied for so many years. Fake news is a big problem. Fake people are a bigger one.**

# 120 PROGRESS AT A SNAIL'S PACE

*Q. What's the difference between a politician and a snail?*

*A. One is slimy, a pest, and leaves a trail everywhere; and the other is a snail.*

**The proliferation of "sliminess," outright fraud, and lies in the political arena during the past ten years has surpassed all that ever preceded it. These policy makers have forsaken the best policies out there: truth and honesty.**

# *Words*

## 121 ANSWER CAREFULLY

*Little Johnny was eating breakfast one morning and got to thinking about things. "Mommy, Mommy, why does Daddy have so few hairs on his head?" he asked.*

*"He thinks a lot," replied his mother, pleased with herself for coming up with a good answer about her husband's baldness.*

*Or at least she thought she was until little Johnny thought it over for a second and then asked, "So why do you have so much hair?"*

**What we say often comes back to haunt us. We would do well to consider the repercussions of our words before we utter them, and at times, keep them to ourselves.**

# *Postscript*

## ETERNALIZATION

*I went to a general store. They wouldn't let me buy anything specific.*

Our acquisitions in life need to be specific if they are to perpetuate. Otherwise we run the risk of living a life of generalities and superficiality never to be internalized. The formula for success is "internalize so that you can eternalize."

# Dear Reader,

I hope you had a good reason to laugh...and a moment or two to reflect.

All the best,

Y.K.

# About the Author

Rabbi Yehoshua Kurland is a popular speaker, a renowned educator, and the bestselling author of *A Time to Dance* about marriage, *A Time to Conceal, a Time to Reveal* about Purim and Chanukah, *Kosher Laughs and Lessons for Life*, volumes 1 and 2, and numerous other books on Jewish thought. Known for using humor as a catalyst for personal growth, Rabbi Kurland was a close student of the renowned Rav Shlomo Freifeld, *zt"l*, and has been a *rebbi* at Yeshiva Sh'or Yoshuv for over four decades.

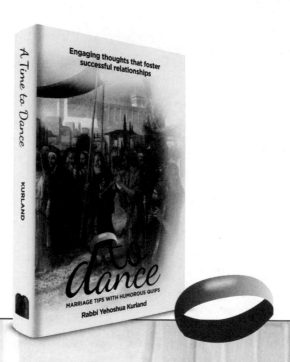

All too often, things get stale.

## How do we find the joy in our marriages once again?

Many words of *mussar* are inevitably distant from us.
We are too delicate and fragile. What works?

Rabbi Yehoshua Kurland's genius lies in his ability
to share deep and powerful messages together
with humorous stories and jokes in the spirit of
the Talmudic *milsa d'bidichusa*.
Through his wit, we become open to his
teachings.
Through his wisdom, we become open to change
and inspiration.
It is time to rediscover *simchah* in our marriages.
It is time to celebrate our lives together and the
symphony of marriage.